BOOKS BY W. S. MERWIN

POEMS

The River Sound 1999
The Folding Cliffs: A Narrative 1998
The Vixen 1996
Travels 1993
Selected Poems 1988
The Rain in the Trees 1988
Opening the Hand 1983
Finding the Islands 1982
The Compass Flower 1977
Writings to an Unfinished Accompaniment 1973
The Carrier of Ladders 1970
The Lice 1967
The Moving Target 1963
The Drunk in the Furnace 1960
Green with Beasts 1956
The Dancing Bears 1954
A Mask for Janus 1952

PROSE

The Lost Upland 1992
Unframed Originals 1982
Houses and Travellers 1977
The Miner's Pale Children 1970

TRANSLATIONS

Sun at Midnight (Poems by Muso Soseki) (WITH SOIKU SHIGEMATSU) 1989
Vertical Poetry (Poems by Roberto Juarroz) 1988
From the Spanish Morning 1985
Four French Plays 1985
Selected Translations 1968–1978 1979
Euripedes' Iphigeneia at Aulis (WITH GEORGE E. DIMOCK, JR.) 1978
Osip Mandelstam, Selected Poems (WITH CLARENCE BROWN) 1974
Asian Figures 1973
Transparence of the World (Poems by Jean Follain) 1969
Voices (Poems of Antonio Porchia) 1969, 1988
Products of the Perfected Civilization (Selected Writings of Chamfort) 1969
Twenty Love Poems and a Song of Despair (Poems by Pablo Neruda) 1969
Selected Translations 1948–1968 1968
The Song of Roland 1963
Lazarillo de Tormes 1962
Spanish Ballads 1961
The Satires of Persius 1960
The Poem of the Cid 1959

ANTHOLOGY

Lament for the Makers: A Memorial Anthology 1996

THE RIVER
SOUND

THE RIVER SOUND

POEMS BY

W. S. MERWIN

ALFRED A. KNOPF NEW YORK

1999

THIS IS A BORZOI BOOK
PUBLISHED BY ALFRED A. KNOPF, INC.

Some of these poems were originally published in the following periodicals:

THE ATLANTIC: *Remembering; Another River; Echoing Light; Shore Birds*
THE BLACK WARRIOR: *Testimony*
FIELD: *Moissac*
THE NATION: *The Wren; Syllables*
THE NEW YORKER: *Chorus; What Is a Garden; Night Turn; 227 Waverly Place; Inauguration; Sheep Passing; Waves in August*
THE NEW YORK TIMES: *The Gardens of Versailles*
THE PARIS REVIEW: *Clear Water; Harm's Way*
POETRY: *Ceremony After an Amputation; The Stranger; A Night Fragrance; Before a Departure in Spring; Sixth Floor Walk-up; Legend; Whoever You Are; The Causeway; The Old Year; Lament for the Makers; Wanting to See; Jeanne Duval; Travelling West at Night; This Time; Left Hand; Late Glimpse; Accompaniment*
SHENANDOAH: *Suite in the Key of Forgetting*
THE YALE REVIEW: *Returns After Dark; The Chinese Mountain Fox; A Claim; That Music*

Lament for the Makers also appears in an anthology of that title published by COUNTERPOINT, Washington, D.C., 1996.

Library of Congress Cataloging-in-Publication Data

Merwin, W. S. (William Stanley), 1927–
   The river sound : poems / by W.S. Merwin.—1st. ed.
     p.   cm.
   ISBN 0-375-40486-4 (hc: alk. paper)
   I. Title.
PS3563.E75R58 1999
811'.54—DC21
                                   98-28255
                                       CIP

Manufactured in the United States of America
First Edition

For Paula

Contents

Contents

THE RIVER
SOUND

CEREMONY AFTER AN AMPUTATION

Spirits of the place who were here before I saw it
 to whom I have made such offerings as I have known how to make
 wanting from the first to approach you with recognition
 bringing for your swept ridge trees lining the wind with seedlings
 that have grown now to become these long wings in chorus
 where the birds assemble and settle their flying lives
 you have taught me without meaning and have lifted me up
 without talk or promise and again and again reappeared to me
 unmistakable and changing and unpronounceable as a face

dust of the time a day in late spring after the silk of rain
 had fallen softly through the night and after the green morning
 the afternoon floating brushed with gold and then the sounds
 of machines erupting across the valley and elbowing up the slopes
 pushing themselves forward to occupy you to be more of you
 who remain the untouched silence through which they are passing
 I try to hear you remembering that we are not separate
 to find you who cannot be lost or elsewhere or incomplete

nature of the solitary machine coming into the story
 from the minds that conceived you and the hands that first conjured up
 the phantom of you in fine lines on the drawing board
 you for whom function is all the good that exists
 you to whom I have come with nothing but purpose
 a purpose of my own as though it was something we shared
 you that were pried from the earth without anyone
 consulting you and were carried off burned beaten metamorphosed
 according to plans and lives to which you owed nothing

let us be at peace with each other let peace be what is between us
 and you now single vanished part of my left hand bit of bone finger-
  end index
 who began with me in the dark that was already my mother
 you who touched whatever I could touch of the beginning
 and were how I touched and who remembered the sense of it
 when I thought I had forgotten it you in whom it waited
 under your only map of one untrodden mountain
 you who did as well as we could through all the hours at the piano
 and who helped undo the bras and found our way to the treasure

and who held the fruit and the pages and knew how to button
    my right cuff and to wash my left ear and had taken in
    heart beats of birds and beloved faces and hair by day and by night
    fur of dogs ears of horses tongues and the latches of doors
    so that I still feel them clearly long after they are gone
    and lake water beside the boat one evening of an ancient summer
    and the vibration of a string over which a bow was moving
    as though the sound of the note were still playing
    and the hand of my wife found in the shallows of waking

you who in a flicker of my inattention
    signalled to me once only my error telling me
    of the sudden blow from the side so that I looked down
    to see not you any longer but instead a mouth
    full of blood calling after you who had already gone gone
    gone ahead into what I cannot know or reach or touch
    leaving in your place only the cloud of pain rising
    into the day filling the light possessing every sound
    becoming the single color and taste and direction

yet as the pain recedes and the moment of it
    you remain with me even in the missing of you
    small boat moving before me on the current under the daylight
    whatever you had touched and had known and took with you
    is with me now as you are when you are already there
    unseen part of me reminding me warning me
    pointing to what I cannot see never letting me forget
    you are my own speaking only to me going with me
    all the rest of the way telling me what is still here

THE STRANGER

(After a Guarani legend recorded by Ernesto Morales)

One day in the forest there was somebody
who had never been there before
it was somebody like the monkeys but taller
and without a tail and without so much hair
standing up and walking on only two feet
and as he went he heard a voice calling Save me

as the stranger looked he could see a snake
a very big snake with a circle of fire
that was dancing all around it
and the snake was trying to get out
but every way it turned the fire was there

so the stranger bent the trunk of a young tree
and climbed out over the fire until he
could hold a branch down to the snake
and the snake wrapped himself around the branch
and the stranger pulled the snake up out of the fire

and as soon as the snake saw that he was free
he twined himself around the stranger
and started to crush the life out of him
but the stranger shouted No No
I am the one who has just saved your life
and you pay me back by trying to kill me

but the snake said I am keeping the law
it is the law that whoever does good
receives evil in return
and he drew his coils tight around the stranger
but the stranger kept on saying No No
I do not believe that is the law

so the snake said I will show you
I will show you three times and you will see
and he kept his coils tight around the stranger's neck
and all around his arms and body
but he let go of the stranger's legs
Now walk he said to the stranger Keep going

so they started out that way and they came
to a river and the river said to them
I do good to everyone and look what they
do to me I save them from dying of thirst
and all they do is stir up the mud
and fill my water with dead things

the snake said One

the stranger said Let us go on and they did
and they came to a carandá-i palm
there were wounds running with sap on its trunk
and the palm tree was moaning I do good
to everyone and look what they do to me
I give them my fruit and my shade and they cut me
and drink from my body until I die

the snake said Two

the stranger said Let us go on and they did
and came to a place where they heard whimpering
and saw a dog with his paw in a basket
and the dog said I did a good thing
and this is what came of it
I found a jaguar who had been hurt
and I took care of him and he got better

and as soon as he had his strength again
he sprang at me wanting to eat me up
I managed to get away but he tore my paw
I hid in a cave until he was gone
and here in this basket I have
a calabash full of milk for my wound
but now I have pushed it too far down to reach

will you help me he said to the snake
and the snake liked milk better than anything
so he slid off the stranger and into the basket
and when he was inside the dog snapped it shut
and swung it against a tree with all his might
again and again until the snake was dead

and after the snake was dead in there
the dog said to the stranger Friend
I have saved your life
and the stranger took the dog home with him
and treated him the way the stranger would treat a dog

THE GARDENS OF VERSAILLES

At what moment can it be said to occur
the grand stillness of this symmetry
whose horizons become the horizon
and whose designer's name seems to be Ours

even when the designer has long since
vanished and the king his master whom
they called The Sun in his day is nobody again
here are the avenues of light reflected

and magnified and here the form's vast claim
to have been true forever as the law
of a universe in which nothing appears
to change and there was nothing before this

except defects of Nature and a waste of marshes
a lake a chaos of birds and wild things
a river making its undirected
way it was always the water that was

motion even while thirty six thousand men
and six thousand horses for more than three
decades diverted it into a thousand
fountains and when all those men and horses

had gone the water flowed on and the sound
of water falling echoes in the dream
the dream of water in which the avenues
all of them are the river on its own way

CHORUS

The wet bamboo clacking in the night rain
crying in the darkness whimpering softly
as the hollow columns touch and slide
along each other swaying with the empty
air these are sounds from before there were voices
gestures older than grief from before there was
pain as we know it the impossibly tall
stems are reaching out groping and waving
before longing as we think of it or loss
as we are acquainted with it or feelings
able to recognize the syllables
that might be their own calling out to them
like names in the dark telling them nothing
about loss or about longing nothing
ever about all that has yet to answer

WHAT IS A GARDEN

All day working happily down near the stream bed
    the light passing into the remote opalescence
it returns to as the year wakes toward winter
    a season of rain in a year already rich
in rain with masked light emerging on all sides
    in the new leaves of the palms quietly waving
time of mud and slipping and of overhearing
    the water under the sloped ground going on whispering
as it travels time of rain thundering at night
    and of rocks rolling and echoing in the torrent
and of looking up after noon through the high branches
    to see fine rain drifting across the sunlight
over the valley that was abused and at last left
    to fill with thickets of rampant aliens
bringing habits but no stories under the mango trees
    already vast as clouds there I keep discovering
beneath the tangle the ancient shaping of water
    to which the light of an hour comes back as to a secret
and there I planted young palms in places I had not pondered
    until then I imagined their roots setting out in the dark
knowing without knowledge I kept trying to see them standing
    in that bend of the valley in the light that would come

A NIGHT FRAGRANCE

Now I am old enough to remember
people speaking of immortality
as though it were something known to exist
a tangible substance that might be acquired
to be used perhaps in the kitchen
every day in whatever was made there
forever after and they applied the word
to literature and the names of things
names of persons and the naming of other
things for them and no doubt they repeated
that word with some element of belief
when they named a genus of somewhat more than
a hundred species of tropical trees and shrubs
some with flowers most fragrant at night
for James Theodore Tabernaemontanus
of Heidelberg physician and botanist
highly regarded in his day over
four centuries ago immortality
might be like that with the scattered species
continuing their various evolutions
the flowers opening by day or night
with no knowledge of bearing a name
of anyone and their fragrance if it
reminds at all not reminding of him

NIGHT TURN

In late summer after the day's heat is over
I walk out after dark into the still garden
wet leaves fragrance of ginger and kamani
the feel of the path underfoot still recalling
a flow of water that found its way long ago
toads are rustling under the lemon trees
looking back I can see through the branches
the light in the kitchen where we were standing
a moment ago in our life together

BEFORE A DEPARTURE IN SPRING

Once more it is April with the first light sifting
    through the young leaves heavy with dew making the colors
remember who they are the new pink of the cinnamon tree
    the gilded lichens of the bamboo the shadowed bronze
of the kamani and the blue day opening
    as the sunlight descends through it all like the return
of a spirit touching without touch and unable
    to believe it is here and here again and awake
reaching out in silence into the cool breath
    of the garden just risen from darkness and days of rain
it is only a moment the birds fly through it calling
    to each other and are gone with their few notes and the flash
of their flight that had vanished before we ever knew it
    we watch without touching any of it and we
can tell ourselves only that this is April this is the morning
    this never happened before and we both remember it

REMEMBERING

There are threads of old sound heard over and over
phrases of Shakespeare or Mozart the slender
wands of the auroras playing out from them
into dark time the passing of a few
migrants high in the night far from the ancient flocks
far from the rest of the words far from the instruments

ANOTHER RIVER

The friends have gone home far up the valley
of that river into whose estuary
the man from England sailed in his own age
in time to catch sight of the late forests
furring in black the remotest edges
of the majestic water always it
appeared to me that he arrived just as
an evening was beginning and toward the end
of summer when the converging surface
lay as a single vast mirror gazing
upward into the pearl light that was
already stained with the first saffron
of sunset on which the high wavering trails
of migrant birds flowed southward as though there were
no end to them the wind had dropped and the tide
and the current for a moment seemed to hang
still in balance and the creaking and knocking
of wood stopped all at once and the known voices
died away and the smells and rocking
and starvation of the voyage had become
a sleep behind them as they lay becalmed
on the reflection of their Half Moon
while the sky blazed and then the time lifted them
up the dark passage they had no name for

ECHOING LIGHT

When I was beginning to read I imagined
that bridges had something to do with birds
and with what seemed to be cages but I knew
that they were not cages it must have been autumn
with the dusty light flashing from the streetcar wires
and those orange places on fire in the pictures
and now indeed it is autumn the clear
days not far from the sea with a small wind nosing
over dry grass that yesterday was green
the empty corn standing trembling and a down
of ghost flowers veiling the ignored fields
and everywhere the colors I cannot take
my eyes from all of them red even the wide streams
red it is the season of migrants
flying at night feeling the turning earth
beneath them and I woke in the city hearing
the call notes of the plover then again and
again before I slept and here far down river
flocking together echoing close to the shore
the longest bridges have opened their slender wings

RETURNS AFTER DARK

Many by now must be
dead the taxi drivers
who sat up before me
twenty even thirty
could it be forty years
ago when no matter
where that time I had gone
if the day was over
and the lights had come on

by the time I could see
the Magellanic Clouds
rise from the black river
and the white circuitry
that ordered us over
the bridge into the crowds
and cliffs of the city
familiar as ever
my life unknown to me

I was beholding it
across another time
each dark facade I thought
looked as it had before
the shining was the same
coming from lives unknown
in other worlds those white
windows burning so far
from the birth of the light

When I have left I imagine they will
repair the window onto the fire escape
that looks north up the avenue clear
to Columbus Circle long I have known
the lights of that valley at every hour
through that unwashed pane and have watched with no
conclusion its river flowing toward me
straight from the featureless distance coming
closer darkening swelling growing distinct
speeding up as it passed below me toward
the tunnel all that time through all that time
taking itself through its sound which became
part of my own before long the unrolling
rumble the iron solos and the sirens
all subsiding in the small hours to voices
echoing from the sidewalks a rustling
in the rushes along banks and the loose
glass vibrated like a remembering bee
as the north wind slipped under the winter sill
at the small table by the window until
my right arm ached and stiffened and I pushed
the chair back against the bed and got up
and went out into the other room that was
filled with the east sky and the day replayed
from the windows and roofs of the Village
the room where friends came and we sat talking
and where we ate and lived together while
the blue paint flurried down from the ceiling
and we listened late with lights out to music
hearing the intercom from the hospital
across the avenue through the Mozart
Dr Kaplan wanted on the tenth floor
while reflected lights flowed backward on the walls

SIXTH FLOOR WALK-UP

Past four in the afternoon the last day here
the winter light is draining out of the sky
to the east over the grays of the roofs
over the tiered bricks and dark water tanks
clock towers aerials penthouse windows
rusted doors bare trees in terrace gardens
in the distance a plane is coming in
lit by the slow burn of the sun sinking
two weeks before the solstice and the lingering
perfect autumn still does not seem to be
gone the walls of the apartment and the long
mirrors are becoming shadows the latest
telephone already cut off is huddled
against the wall with its deaf predecessors
the movers have not showed up for what is left
bare bed bare tables and the sofa the piled
LP's the great chair from which at this hour
once I called up a friend on Morton Street
to tell him that all the windows facing
west down the avenue were reflecting
a red building flaming like a torch
somewhere over near the old post office
on Christopher Street the sirens were converging
all the bells clanging and the sky was clear
as it is now they are stacking Christmas trees
along the fence again down at the corner
to the music of the subway under
the avenue on its way to Brooklyn
twenty-five years

LEGEND

Our own city had the second highest
VD rate in the country yielding
only to Hagerstown Maryland
we boasted aged somewhere around eleven
taking credit for it thinking we might
even be first it was fundamental
knowledge closer to home than the famous
roller coaster down at Rocky Glen
which we agreed was one of the world's
most dangerous with its hairpin trestle
out over water and the whole thing
about to collapse a lady got on
back in the summer with a baby
and when they got off the baby was dead
but the steady aura of the unspeakable
emanated from figures like Jennie
Dee the reigning madam whom we had not seen
but we all knew she rode in a chauffeur-driven
black Cadillac with flags on the fenders
and was friends with the mayor the Chamber
of Commerce and the police it was a mile
exactly to the courthouse downtown
by the short cut over the embankment
and along the weedy right-of-way to the iron
truss across the already stove-black
Lackawanna drunks who fell in there
were known to be blown-up and all shades of blue
by the time they were fished out on the South Side
the paint was worn off the top of the truss
where we ran across it into the smell
of the gasworks which haunted us part way
up the steep cobbles past the one gray house
all by itself with its shades drawn tight
and lights on in the daytime we never
saw anyone go in or come out of there
two dollars to the best of our belief
on the far side of the street whispering
through the cold echoes under the railroad bridge

CLEAR WATER

Once a child's poem began a pond of time
what followed must have flowed from what a child

remembered in time about a child
he had once been except that the poem

began in a time before the poem
and before the pond that the child remembered

once a child's pond began a remembered
time that a child followed until the pond

was the time a poem began with a pond
that a child thought he remembered once not flowing

but by the time the poem began it was flowing
once upon the memory of a child

whose poem began before he was a child
a murmur flowing from before he began

though what he remembered once began
with the poem on the pond of a child's time

a child began a poem once in a time
remembered with a pond that he had seen

flowing from a spring he had never seen
kept by an unseen giant who once was a child

whose name was Mimir before the child
began the poem once in remembered time

the giant keeps the beginning before time
in the spring of mourning under the pond of time

HARM'S WAY

How did someone come at last to the word for patience
and know that it was the right word or patience

the sounds had come such a distance from the will to give pain
which that person kept like a word for patience

the word came on in its own time like a star
at such a distance from either pain or patience

it echoed someone in a mirror who threatened with fire
an immortal with no bounds of hatred or patience

the syllables were uttered out of the sound of fire
but in silence they became the word for patience

it is not what the hawk hangs on or the hushed fox
waits with who do not need a word for patience

passing through the sound of another's pain
it brings with it something of that pain or patience

but how did whoever first came to it convey
to anyone else that it was the word for patience

they must have arrived at other words by then
to be able to use something from pain for patience

there is no such word in the ages of the leaves
in the days of the grass there is no name for patience

many must have travelled the whole way without knowing
that what they wanted was the word for patience

it is as far from patience as William is from me
and yet known to be patience the word for patience

WHOEVER YOU ARE

By now when you say *I stop somewhere waiting for you*
who is the I and who come to that is you

there are those words that were written a long time ago
by someone I have read about who they assure me is you

the handwriting is still running over the pages
but the one who has disappeared from the script is you

I wonder what age you were when those words came to you
though I think it is not any age at all that is you

stopping and waiting under the soles of my feet
this morning this waking this looking up is you

but nothing has stopped in fact and I do not know
what is waiting and surely that also is you

every time you say it you seem to be speaking
through me to some me not yet there who I suppose is you

you said you were stopping and waiting before I was here
maybe the one I heard say it then is you

THE CAUSEWAY

This is the bridge where at dusk they hear voices
far out in the meres and marshes or they say they hear voices

the bridge shakes and no one else is crossing at this hour
somewhere along here is where they hear voices

this is the only bridge though it keeps changing
from which some always say they hear voices

the sounds pronounce an older utterance out of the shadows
sometimes stifled sometimes carried from clear voices

what can be recognized in the archaic syllables
frightens many and tells others not to fear voices

travellers crossing the bridge have forgotten where they were going
in a passage between the remote and the near voices

there is a tale by now of a bridge a long time before this one
already old before the speech of our day and the mere voices

when the Goths were leaving their last kingdom in Scythia
they could feel the bridge shaking under their voices

the bank and the first spans are soon lost to sight
there seemed no end to the horses carts people and all their voices

in the mists at dusk the whole bridge sank under them
into the meres and marshes leaving nothing but their voices

they are still speaking the language of their last kingdom
that no one remembers who now hears their voices

whatever translates from those rags of sound
persuades some who hear them that they are familiar voices

grandparents never seen ancestors in their childhoods
now along the present bridge they sound like dear voices

some may have spoken in my own name in an earlier language
when last they drew breath in the kingdom of their voices

THE CHINESE MOUNTAIN FOX

Now we can tell that there
must once have been a time
when it was always there
and might at any time

appear out of nowhere
as they were wont to say
and probably to their
age it did look that way

though how are we to say
from the less than certain
evidence of our day
and they referred often

through the centuries when
it may have been a sight
they considered common
so that they mentioned it

as a presence they were
sure everyone had seen
and would think familiar
they alluded even

then until it became
their unquestioned habit
like a part of the name
to that element it

had of complete surprise
of being suddenly
the blaze in widened eyes
that had been turned only

at that moment upon
some place quite near that they
all through their lives had known
and passed by every day

perhaps at the same place
where they themselves had just
been standing that live face
looking as though it must

have been following them
would have appeared with no
warning they could fathom
or ever come to know

though they made studied use
of whatever system
logic calculus ruse
they trusted in their time

to tell them where they might
count on it next and when
if once they figured right
as though it travelled in

a pattern they could track
like the route of some far
light in the zodiac
comet or migrant star

but it was never where
they had thought it would be
and showed the best of their
beliefs successively

to be without substance
shadows they used to cast
old tales and illusions
out of some wishful past

each in turn was consigned
to the role of legend
while yet another kind
of legend had wakened

to play the animal
even while it was there
the unpredictable
still untaken creature

part lightning and part rust
the fiction was passed down
with undiminished trust
while the sightings began

to be unusual
second-hand dubious
unverifiable
turning to ghost stories

all the more easily
since when it had been seen
most times that was only
by someone all alone

and unlike its cousins
of the lowlands captive
all these generations
and kept that way alive

never had it been caught
poisoned or hunted down
by packs of dogs or shot
hung up mounted or worn

never even been seen
twice by the same person
in the place it had been
when they looked there again

and whatever they told
of it as long as they
still spoke of it revealed
always more of the way

they looked upon the light
while it was theirs to see
and what they thought it might
let them glimpse at any

moment than of the life
that they had rarely been
able to catch sight of
in an instant between

now and where it had been
at large before they came
when the mountains were green
before it had a name

THE OLD YEAR

I remember the light
at the end of one year
the gold mist is still bright
thousands of miles from here

and voices are calling
across the steep meadows
until the late falling
asleep of their echoes

less than a breath before
the silence where they are
the bare veined limbs are more
clear than ever but far

out of reach as always
lit by a new distance
and its beam that catches
the ring of last moments

I have stayed up to see
each time they are farther
than I thought they would be
one after another

those occasions that I
was to be happy in
while they were passing by
as I knew even then

they are farther away
once more the glimpses of
the sun one winter day
the eyes of early love

city after city
frozen in the night sky
each deafening party
spinning as the sparks fly

they appear in a new
perspective of absence
that each was led into
and the good rooms that once

upon a time have been
each in its turn the heart
of a whole horizon
have been taken apart

emptied and finally
left out in the cold air
to be recalled only
as dreams of what they were

what we dream now is here
the hours that we forget
in the garden the clear
leaf light after sunset

in the dream we believe
the house sails on the hill
it never means to leave
and the winter moon still

floats on its lucid bay
in the life where we met
and the year and the day
have not gone from us yet

LAMENT FOR THE MAKERS

I that all through my early days
I remember well was always
    the youngest of the company
    save for one sister after me

from the time when I was able
to walk under the dinner table
    and be punished for that promptly
    because its leaves could fall on me

father and mother overhead
who they talked with and what they said
    were mostly clouds that knew already
    directions far too old for me

at school I skipped a grade so that
whatever I did after that
    each year everyone would be
    older and hold it up to me

at college many of my friends
were returning veterans
    equipped with an authority
    I admired and they treated me

as the kid some years below them
so I married half to show them
    and listened with new vanity
    when I heard it said of me

how young I was and what a shock
I was the youngest on the block
    I thought I had it coming to me
    and I believe it mattered to me

and seemed my own and there to stay
for a while then came the day
    I was in another country
    other older friends around me

my youth by then taken for granted
and found that it had been supplanted
 the notes in some anthology
 listed persons born after me

how long had that been going on
how could I be not quite so young
 and not notice and nobody
 even bother to inform me

though my fond hopes were taking longer
than I had hoped when I was younger
 a phrase that came more frequently
 to suggest itself to me

but the secret was still there
safe in the unprotected air
 that breath that in its own words only
 sang when I was a child to me

and caught me helpless to convey it
with nothing but the words to say it
 though it was those words completely
 and they rang it was clear to me

with a changeless overtone
I have listened for since then
 hearing that note endlessly
 vary every time beyond me

trying to find where it comes from
and to what words it may come
 and forever after be
 present for the thought kept at me

that my mother and every day
of our lives would slip away
 like the summer and suddenly
 all would have been taken from me

but that presence I had known
sometimes in words would not be gone
    and if it spoke even once for me
    it would stay there and be me

however few might choose those words
for listening to afterwards
    there I would be awake to see
    a world that looked unchanged to me

I suppose that was what I thought
young as I was then and that note
    sang from the words of somebody
    in my twenties I looked around me

to all the poets who were then
living and whose lines had been
    sustenance and company
    and a light for years to me

I found the portraits of their faces
first in the rows of oval spaces
    in Oscar Williams' *Treasury*
    so they were settled long before me

and they would always be the same
in that distance of their fame
    affixed in immortality
    during their lifetimes while around me

all was woods seen from a train
no sooner glimpsed than gone again
    but those immortals constantly
    in some measure reassured me

then first there was Dylan Thomas
from the White Horse taken from us
    to the brick wall I woke to see
    for years across the street from me

then word of the death of Stevens
brought a new knowledge of silence
    the nothing not there finally
    the sparrow saying Bethou me

how long his long auroras had
played on the darkness overhead
    since I looked up from my Shelley
    and Arrowsmith first showed him to me

and not long from his death until
Edwin Muir had fallen still
    that fine bell of the latter day
    not well heard yet it seems to me

Sylvia Plath then took her own
direction into the unknown
    from her last stars and poetry
    in the house a few blocks from me

Williams a little afterwards
was carried off by the black rapids
    that flowed through Paterson as he
    said and their rushing sound is in me

that was the time that gathered Frost
into the dark where he was lost
    to us but from too far to see
    his voice keeps coming back to me

then the sudden news that Ted
Roethke had been found floating dead
    in someone's pool at night but he
    still rises from his lines for me

MacNeice watched the cold light harden
when that day had left the garden
    stepped into the dark ground to see
    where it went but never told me

and on the rimless wheel in turn
Eliot spun and Jarrell was borne
    off by a car who had loved to see
    the racetrack then there came to me

one day the knocking at the garden
door and the news that Berryman
    from the bridge had leapt who twenty
    years before had quoted to me

the passage where *a jest* wrote Crane
falls from the speechless caravan
    with a wave to bones and Henry
    and to all that he had told me

I dreamed that Auden sat up in bed
but I could not catch what he said
    by that time he was already
    dead someone next morning told me

and Marianne Moore entered the ark
Pound would say no more from the dark
    who once had helped to set me free
    I thought of the prose around me

and David Jones would rest until
the turn of time under the hill
    but from the sleep of Arthur he
    wakes an echo that follows me

Lowell thought the shadow skyline
coming toward him was Manhattan
    but it blacked out in the taxi
    once he read his *Notebook* to me

at the number he had uttered
to the driver a last word
    then that watchful and most lonely
    wanderer whose words went with me

everywhere Elizabeth
Bishop lay alone in death
    they were leaving the party early
    our elders it came home to me

but the needle moved among us
taking always by surprise
    flicking by too fast to see
    to touch a friend born after me

and James Wright by his darkened river
heard the night heron pass over
    took his candle down the frosty
    road and disappeared before me

Howard Moss had felt the gnawing
at his name and found that nothing
    made it better he was funny
    even so about it to me

Graves in his nineties lost the score
forgot that he had died before
    found his way back innocently
    who once had been a guide to me

Nemerov sadder than his verse
said a new year could not be worse
    then the black flukes of agony
    went down leaving the words with me

Stafford watched his hand catch the light
seeing that it was time to write
    a memento of their story
    signed and is a plain before me

now Jimmy Merrill's voice is heard
like an aria afterward
    and we know he will never be
    old after all who spoke to me

on the cold street that last evening
of his heart that leapt at finding
    some yet unknown poetry
    then waved through the window to me

in that city we were born in
one by one they have all gone
    out of the time and language we
    had in common which have brought me

to this season after them
the best words did not keep them from
    leaving themselves finally
    as this day is going from me

and the clear note they were hearing
never promised anything
    but the true sound of brevity
    that will go on after me

SUITE IN THE KEY OF FORGETTING

You remember surely
is the way it begins
in a time afterwards
far from the beginning
which no one remembers

remember that story
of Nerval's beginning
away on a journey
one year in Germany
in some river city
Cologne or Frankfurt if
I remember rightly
Frankfurt surely and he
gave the year precisely
as it occurs to me
though only its number
if indeed I am not
inventing after all

though that date must have been
fixed in his memory
like the year of a scar
loss or discovery
from his mid-century
which by now is only
a flutter in the words
for all that was flying then
through the echoing hall

but as you recall he
explored the boulevards
and offerings of that
brimming metropolis
and stood in the market
of furs staring at what
had been stripped from the lives
of the white bear that woke
in the kingdom of white
the blue fox that journeyed

like a day in daylight
I thought of them again
one evening in Paris
more than a century
later when a spotlit
furrier's shop flaunted
twelve infant sables ranged
with mouths locked on a gold
collar I remember
who was with me and what
year it was that summer
but not where we went then
after those skins were passed
it seems to me he came
to the racks of old books
dark backs closed on themselves
standing among strangers
no longer wanted by
part of their own story
some name on the flyleaf
with a date and an Ex
Libris in that city
well known for its freedom
to publish so that lives
histories and journals
memoirs from anywhere
might have ended up there

he had already bought
more than he should have but
still he could not resist
wandering through others
and came at last to one
written half in German
half in French recounting
so the title page claimed
the extraordinary
history of the Count
and Abbé of Bucquoy
with the remarkable

details of his escape
from the prisons of Fort
l'Évêque and the Bastille
along with several works
of his in verse and prose
and particularly
the *game* of women and
was that the English word
game some affectation
already out of date
or was it a misprint
for the French gamme or scale
like the English gamut
rooted in the lowest
note of the hexachord
chanted in Latin to
St John the Baptist one
tongue or the other came
to a like suggestion
and the uncertainty
in the language as he
read it might have warned him
of untrustworthy ground
and evasions to come
but that escaped me too
when I read in my turn
and even when it came
to mind long afterwards
the bookseller wanted
what sounded like too much
for that book or at least
more than he felt he should
spend by that time and he
told himself he would find
the volume easily
in Paris and took down
title and publisher
and where the opus had
first been offered for sale
a century and more

before though again he
might have noticed the light
insubstance of the names
Jean de la France vendor
at Good Faith an address
in Hope he copied it
all and in good faith left

do you remember as
he had asked Daphne once
thinking of Octavie
do you remember that
song that begins again
always begins again
under the sycamore
under the white laurels
or the trembling willows
that song of love do you
remember the temple
he was recalling her
face as she stood before
the great columns the marks
of her teeth in the skins
of the bitter lemons
the cave of the dragon's
seed and the quaking of
promise the promises
do you remember

how it went after he
woke in Paris again
and there set out to find
that same book in a time
much restricted of late
by the censor in all
fiction written to be
continued but he told
himself that his subject
was in fact history
and when asked for a name

he said the Abbé of
Bucquoy imagining
there in the capital
turning up in no time
the documentation
for this personage who
once had been flesh and blood
there was the book itself
more than once listed in
France though said to be rare
but surely somewhere in
a public library
private collection or
specialist's cabinet
he was sure he recalled
clearly what he had read
of the Abbé's story
from the volume that he
had not bought in Frankfurt
and he had found the same
details of the Abbé's
adventures in Madame
Dunoyer's witty and
curious letters though
they spoke at a remove
and under the new law
it would be ruinous
to recount those events
without the Abbé's own
words for confirmation
particularly in
a country where persons
who possessed power or
the pretense of power
were certain to use it

you would be wise a friend
told him not to rely
upon Madame's letters
for your authority

wait for the National
Library to open
on October the first
there on the day the name
of the book after some
time was discovered but
not the book and they said
come back in three days and
they had not found it then
it may be in among
the novels they told him

novels he cried but this
is history itself
it tells of the revolt
of the Camisards and
the Protestants going
into exile the league
of Lorraine and Mandrin
raising his army there
to take Beaune and Dijon
yes the librarian
said I know but the wrongs
of the past were made at
different times and they
can be put right only
one by one and upon
particular request
no one can help you here
but Monsieur Ravenal
and unfortunately
he is not in this week

came the Monday and yes
Monsieur Ravenal was
there in the reading room
and the person of whom
the inquiry was made
actually knew him
and offered to provide

an introduction which
could not have been received
with greater courtesy
I am enchanted he
said to meet you and I
ask you but to grant me
a few days before I
devote myself to your
interest for I am
this week at the bidding
of the public and now
we have been introduced
you have become you see
a private acquaintance

which could not be denied
he considered the room
and the public from whom
he had been set aside
watching distinguished but
impoverished scholars
providing six hundred
quotidian readers
with the usual fare
and those who had come there
to get out of the cold
and sleep safe in a chair
endangering such books
as fell into their hands
ordinary idlers
retired bourgeois salesmen
presently unemployed
widowers copyists
ancient lunatics such
as that poor Carnaval
who appeared every day
clad in red or sky blue
or apple green and crowned
with a wreath of flowers
he remembered them all

out of earlier times
other days of his own
he watched them tearing out
pages poring over
columns of addresses
none had given a name

and from this library
he knew that some volume
with no other of its
kind in the world vanished
almost daily and went
unmissed for a while that
single survivor that
sole testimony gone
he thought of the burning
of the library in
Alexandria and
not by Islam but by
his sainted ancestors
he was writing it all
to the Director of
the National and he
was remembering as
he wrote it another
visit to Frankfurt years
earlier and the lives
he was looking for then

that was the first letter
of twelve and whose was this
charmed hand writing it down
only from memory
was it our poor Gérard
whom the men of science
as his unfeeling friend
Dumas repeated it
had pronounced sick and in
need of treatment whereas
for us Alexandre

said his stories his dreams
are better than ever
at one time he will be
Sultain Ghera Gherai
Duke of Egypt or Count
of Abyssinia
Baron of Smyrna and
write a letter to my
supreme authority
requesting permission
to declare war upon
Emperor Nicolas
or did the hand belong
to someone whom Dumas
had never laid eyes on

whose efforts to summon
that memoir of Bucquoy
from the forest of shades
drew him from library
to library and on
to the ruins of stone
set upon stone to keep
some memory alive
the bones of a chateau
eyeless its library
gone the tomb of Rousseau
and a family tree
ancient vast unlikely
and part of another
journal or memoir by
a beautiful ill-starred
forbear of the Abbé
or so-called Abbé as
some reference put it
she must have been the one
he had been trying to
remember the whole way

what he found was perhaps
a hundred pages in
her own hand the paper
foxed the ink ghostly her
name had been Angélique
the Count's daughter who cared
neither for jewels nor
adornments longing for
death to still her longing
until love came to her
and misfortune seized her
following her until
she was alone and with
nothing to cover her
nakedness and no one
knew what became of her

what did become of her
she was not in her name
given to the story
not in whatever he
could remember of her
not in her own words
that enchanted melting
being impossible
to hold or to believe

TESTIMONY

The year I will be seventy
who never could believe my age
still foolish it appears to me
as I have been at every stage
but not beyond the average
I trust nor yet arrived at such
wisdom as might view the damage
without regretting it too much

though I have sipped the rim by now
of trouble and should know the taste
I am not certain as to how
the pain of learning what is lost
is transformed into light at last
some it illumines from their birth
and some will hunger to the last
for the moment and hands of earth

while some apparently would give
the open unrepeatable
present in which they wake and live
to glimpse a place where they were small
or in love once and be able
to capture in that second sight
what in the plain original
they missed and this time get it right

they would know how to hold it there
a still life still alive and know
what to do with it now and where
to hang it and how not to go
from there again perhaps although
when they were living in its day
they could not wait for it to go
and were dying to get away

and at one time or another
some have tied themselves tight to cling
desperately as though they were
in white water and near drowning
onto in fact the very thing
they most wanted to be rid of
hanging on despite everything
to their anguish and only love

the shell games move around the block
one where a crowd is always drawn
promises a time off the clock
at any moment to the one
who is smart enough to put down
the present hour and calculate
what it will be worth later on
and meanwhile hold the breath and wait

hope lingers with its dear advice
that gets to each in different ways
growing up means you sacrifice
what you like now knowing it pays
with champagne in the holidays
and comforts that are meant to stay
and come to that as the man says
what is the present anyway

and I of course am taken in
by each of them repeatedly
whatever words I may have been
using since I have used any
reached me out of a memory
on the way to some plan or promise
not yet there and after many
notices I have come to this

what is it then I hear the same
linnet notes in the morning air
that I heard playing when I came
now the new light has reached to
where
the pleated leaves are holding their
hands out to it without moving
and as the young day fills them there
I am the child still listening

who from a farmhouse once in spring
walked out in the long day alone
through old apple orchards climbing
to a hilltop where he looked down
into a green valley that shone
with such light all the words were poor
later to tell what he had known
they said that was the night pasture

I am the child who plans the Ark
back of the house while there is still
time and rides bareback on the dark
horse through the summer night until
day finds us on the leafless hill
who stands at evening by the lake
looking out on it as I will
as long as I am here awake

to see the coming of the day
here once more that comes once only
I am new to it the same way
I was when it first dawned on me
no one else has turned into me
under the clothes that I have worn
I know that I am the same me
that I have been since I was born

the boats do not appear to be
any farther on the river
they shine passing as silently
through the bright sunlight as ever
I am at the window over
the Palisades where I look down
the back wall of the church over
the viaduct and Hoboken

never suspecting that this may
be the one time it will happen
my father asking me today
whatever his thought may have been
if I will promise that I can
be quiet if I go along
and stay with him while he works on
his sermon and my promising

the keys ring at the heavy door
the old skin of varnish opens
our feet echo on the sloped floor
down dark aisles to the green curtains
of the chancel and our outlines
flicker along the sunbeams through
the deep underwater silence
of this sleep we have waked into

stairs circle to the high window
where as I kneel to watch the bright
river I hear behind me Thou
fool and then the typewriter write
and stop and him repeat This night
under his breath with certainty
again Thou fool again This night
shall thy soul be required of thee

but I pretend I do not hear
I know that he is speaking to
somebody who is never here
I keep looking out the window
the boats that I can see there no
longer ply the living water
the room his words are spoken to
long ago vanished into air

how many years since we lived there
we were told after we had gone
the church was sold in bad repair
to stand empty and be torn down
soon and the place where it had been
and the long grass knew it no more
no stone was left upon a stone
trees climbed out of the ruined floor

stretching their shadows up the wall
of the long brick apartment house
next door until they entered all
the stories of the south windows
children were brought up inside those
frames with the branches always there
families behind those shadows
have grown and moved away somewhere

after whole lives at that address
during which they have never seen
the place without its squatter trees
poplars and the scorned common one
that some call the tree of heaven
wars have dragged on and faded since
the last neighbors have forgotten
that anything else stood there once

and in a few months it will be
since the night my father died
a quarter of a century
as time is numbered on this side
the rain then sluicing down outside
past midnight and the hour of one
I came in from the street and dried
and never heard the telephone

and after I had gone to bed
to lie listening while the rain
beat on the roof above my head
and watch the lights reflected on
the blue ceiling turning again
backward I heard the door open
my closest friend had braved the rain
with the message that he was gone

only a little while before
maybe an hour or so since they
had tried to call me and not more
than a few minutes either way
from where the clocks had stood they say
when I was born perhaps we passed
that close and missed in the same way
it used to happen in the past

whoever was he talking to
back when he spoke to me and when
I heard his voice as I still do
though now the words are almost gone
who do I hear that I heard then
as in those moments when he would
tell something about Rimerton
in the train smoke of his childhood

looking onto the Erie tracks
in front and from the rear windows
down the steep bank below the backs
of the jacked houses and their rows
of cabbages and potatoes
in summer to the ragged line
past which the later river flows
on after all of them have gone

he made it sound as though it was
a garden since it had been lost
some glow of a distant promise
colored the words he favored most
for the age when they were poorest
his mother with seven children
who had survived he was the last
she kept them upright on her own

after the man who married her
and fathered them had taken off
working his way down the river
to Pittsburgh and the city life
they said he drank which was enough
for most of them to tell of him
nobody played Hail To The Chief
when my grandfather made it home

hers were the threads in which they all
were sewn and they had made of her
an ancient on a pedestal
before I can remember her
established in her rocking chair
with her Bible by the window
her needle pausing in the air
little more would I ever know

except in remnants handed down
as patchwork through the family
none of them telling how her own
life unfurled but for one early
glimpse of the time she waved good-bye
too small to know what it was for
as the young men went marching by
on their way to the Civil War

they could repeat it back to her
didn't you Mumma they would say
wave good-bye to them remember
for company get her to say
what she could tell about that day
being held up high at the gate
and she would laugh and look away
with nothing further to relate

the very way my father and
the rest of them persistently
told no more of what had happened
than their old favorites and he
never went on with a story
he began and any question
would extinguish it completely
so what was past was past and gone

that cold summer after he died
my mother each time anyone
asked what she would do now replied
that she would live on there alone
all of the garden beds were sown
she liked to be out in the air
taking care of them on her own
some told her she would die out there

fall over and be found some day
and she would nod and say that she
could not think of a better way
to go and laugh at that but she
meant what she said as they could see
some remembered then her saying
when the subject came up that she
never was afraid of dying

when had she first felt that was so
her father died when she was four
from then on she would never know
what she knew of him any more
was it he she had seen before
and his eyes with the day inside
going away already or
was all that after he had died

out of the remnants in her head
made up of what she had been told
after that minute by the bed
and her closed eyes close to the cold
forehead with nothing she could hold
tight and believe that it was him
all the pictures of him looked old
and not one of them looked like him

but things were there instead of him
papers he had once written on
clothes he had worn turned into him
in the days when the shades were down
and the black butterfly hung on
the door to tell the street to mourn
and the box was lying open
under the room where she was born

in the house in Colorado
Denver the glint of promise where
the doctors told him he should go
repeating that the mountain air
perhaps and their words trailed off there
he might go on inspecting for
the railroads just as well out there
hope had been what they came out for

the train was carrying the night
back it kept beating in her mind
keeping time with the thread of light
around what the man called the blind
one of the strangers being kind
she felt her mother lying warm
beside her and reached out to find
the wrapped bird of her brother's arm

they were already far away
in a place they would never know
rolling a darkness through its day
all of it would be long ago
when she woke up in Ohio
which she had never seen but where
everyone spoke to her as though
she had always been living there

and known the bedroom and the bed
that her mother had always known
and the house that her mother said
had been hers until she had grown
and married it still seemed her own
my mother thought that it must be
familiar from the names alone
all that she had just come to see

there were no mountains any more
it seemed they had been forgotten
her brother Morris said they were
still there over the horizon
and the gods too through whose garden
she had heard that they had wheeled her
in her carriage in the hidden
time before she could remember

when next she woke there was the black
city Pittsburgh tight around her
she prayed they might be taken back
to the house above the river
in Ohio where her father
was born it was called Cheshire there
they had stayed with her grandfather
why could they not be living there

some day they might her mother said
but for now they would have to be
here she spoke of their daily bread
since all the insurance money
had been lost and it was only
here that she could earn a living
for them and her own family
was their home for the time being

and they visited Ohio
sometimes through that next summer when
her mother did not seem to know
how sick she had become by then
there in the foreground of the brown
photographs she is the shadow
taking pictures of her children
the sun hats and the wide hair bow

the white horse and the garden swing
the summer was not even done
and the heat when she lay dying
all the shades drawn and everyone
whispering in the corner on
the landing passing the word pain
back and forth then the bending down
to kiss her and she too was gone

and everyone in black again
the shaken veils still whispering
what will happen to the children
how could she bear such suffering
a few of them remembering
how beautiful she used to be
and remained so through everything
until this marked her finally

and it was Pittsburgh after that
brought up by her mother's mother
assured that they were fortunate
to be fed clothed and together
in one house after another
with no one in the family
uncles aunts or her grandmother
able to hang onto money

maybe her mother would have been
able to keep things in order
the work that she had found had been
with figures as a bookkeeper
at the Woman's Exchange and her
hand was elegant and even
with a clear grace that my mother
kept in mind when she held a pen

she loathed it from the day she went
to Shakespeare School Morris did too
she hated every day she spent
in the house on Penn Avenue
doubly so from the time she knew
one aunt her mother's sister Ride
baptized Marie had moved in too
shortly after her mother died

Ride then was getting a divorce
from Uncle Jack and they heard Ride
insist it was his fault of course
but they were making him provide
at least after the way he lied
and ran around behind her back
as she talked they could hear his side
everyone had liked Uncle Jack

my mother young as she was then
considered Ride haughty and vain
later she thought she might have been
unjust to her but it was plain
she felt Ride had been blessed in vain
with that life they had together
and had thrown it away again
a gift not good enough for her

while my mother kept thinking of
what she had known of her parents
whom she was sure had been in love
how they had clung to every chance
so that even in their absence
she felt what they had tried to hold
as it was slipping through their hands
and none of that could have been told

not that she ever would have said
a word about it anyway
she would carry it in her head
like a number that knew its way
to the next column of the day
making a shorthand as she went
that none could read and she would say
no one would know what she had meant

she was determined that she would
leave no loose end whatever she
might have to do she would be good
at school quiet and orderly
all the homework done perfectly
piano lessons practised long
and the fine seams finished neatly
so that there would be nothing wrong

but if only her mother lived
she liked to think that maybe they
by some miracle might have moved
to Ohio again one day
before too long and they could stay
near Aunt Susan she could recall
sometimes hearing her mother say
that that would be congenial

there were the cousins whom she knew
Sam and Minerva and she ran
down the list of the others who
lived near there she could see each one
and remember when she had gone
to visit them and play beside
the river in the summer sun
then one day her grandmother died

that was death in a different place
it burned to tell her she had been
wanting in gratitude and grace
toward the shade of this short woman
who had taken all of them in
by turns until they said her door
never could keep out anyone
so she took boarders and stayed poor

Morris had moved out and found work
still nursing dreams of college but
from his salary as a clerk
at the railroad office he brought
my mother an allowance that
he paid until he had made sure
her own wages were adequate
though scarcely to take of her

she was the star secretary
at North Church and awakened there
the ardor of that seminary
student who drove the preacher's car
anyone would have noticed her
beautiful as she was by then
you can still see in a picture
a shadowy reproduction

her mother's beauty there again
some agreed who remembered that
Morris did not deny it when
they would say that and he heard it
he could see what made them say it
but did not believe either one
looked like the other no he thought
neither resembled anyone

she and the optimistic young
man driving toward the ministry
stepped out together before long
theater and boating party
outings in someone's Model T
and then the ring and planning for
the wedding Morris would just see
when he died she was twenty-four

her mother's will in pencil had
not half filled a folded paper
so small that it might have drifted
out of one world through another
unnoticed saying she would rather
one had her broach and one a ring
after those were taken from her
to leave her without anything

Morris had a way of reading
lost to everything around him
one valve in his heart was bleeding
they had known of that for some time
before long he could scarcely climb
the front steps without breathing hard
then there was nothing left of him
his blanket his library card

and of her father there was this
imitation alligator
case clasping the full deck of his
passes as railroad inspector
none good for transit any more
none anyway transferable
no one she knew had set out for
most stations on the timetable

all three had seen while they were young
blankness arriving through the day
it followed as they moved among
others it never went away
there was nothing they knew to say
but the same words the others said
in church closing their eyes to pray
and seeing nothing just ahead

and she had seen them watching it
known its reflection in their eyes
every time recognizing what
was not there every time it was
the same unaltering surprise
while each in turn had told her they
believed in that which never dies
and will be there again one day

and she believed it in the words
so familiar they must be true
she said them over afterwards
in those days as she used to do
when she was small before she knew
why they were said time after time
or what they were referring to
she would understand that in time

the same words in other voices
were all waiting in the country
when they moved to the first churches
Yatesborough and Rural Valley
to stand in the cemetery
and hear the praying as before
and to sing of the day when we
shall meet on that beautiful shore

by and by but it seemed to be
a truth without a face like air
while she saw her own dead plainly
they appeared in her mind somewhere
close to her always waiting there
outside what the words were saying
in the third year of marriage their
first child signalled it was coming

it was hard for her to believe
that a new life was on the way
to her who had grown up to grieve
for lives in turn taken away
as one after another they
had left her for that absent place
might a life come to her and stay
she could see nothing of its face

but with the year turning in her
she wrote a letter out ahead
to the unseen in case she were
not to stay with you as she said
so you might be sure she wanted
you from the moment that she knew
you were there she had not needed
to know more than that about you

the illusion of testaments
so careful and so shrewdly planned
so finely tuned their instruments
so often reconsidered and
words and characters realigned
to determine a future where
the here and now will understand
what they have coming to them there

cards change before they can be played
at times only the words stay on
long after everything they said
and had provided for is gone
while the mansions like bread upon
the waters become history
whole writings come to light again
saying what was supposed to be

when the cold year was dark and young
their child was born whom she would say
whenever that bell had been rung
had been perfect in every way
it was a boy and she said they
informed her he was beautiful
but they had taken him away
before she had seen him at all

and then it never would be clear
why within minutes he was dead
when he had scarcely wakened here
a rush of blood into the head
was the cause of it so they said
but was that from some injury
at birth or mishap afterward
nobody would tell that story

if it turned out to be a son
she meant to name him for her father
and so they did when he was gone
and then both were gone together
by the same name and years later
I was to be the son who read
the clipped notice and her letter
but only after she was dead

those were her deaths before my day
by that time she could turn to hear
outside the voices on her way
a stillness only partly here
and whatever she would hold dear
giving herself up to its care
she looked beyond it without fear
toward what she felt was waiting there

with my father I could not tell
what after all death meant for him
I heard him at one funeral
after another on that theme
preaching of heaven from the time
the smell of flowers frightened me
in a school friend's living room
as they drew me past the body

I knew the words he always said
which others had taught him to say
in that voice he put on to read
from scripture and said Let us pray
he told me that death came the way
sleep brought quiet to our bodies
we could not see what went away
but what was buried fed the trees

it did not sound as good to me
as he was telling me it was
I hoped that it would never be
and I would not get to that place
myself but would be me always
he told me that we all grow tired
at last and will be glad for peace
that waits for us as a reward

how much of that did he believe
where were those answers coming from
were they what he was certain of
in his own body all the time
alone travelling sick with some
nameless humiliating ill
when he kept asking to go home
out of the veterans' hospital

these nights that we see the comet
in the northwest as the stars come
saying the name we have for it
now which is nothing like its name
in lost languages the last time
it could be seen from where we are
thousands of years ago our name
of which it remains unaware

as it will be when next it swims
into what eye may then be here
after our knowledge and our hymns
draw the tail of their vanished sphere
on through an unremembered year
I think of how I thought of him
then in myself and tried to hear
his sounding of what was to come

after the words of ringing text
youthful hopes and dawns of promise
the sleepless gnawing that came next
in a row of empty churches
marriage heading in separate ways
children growing into distance
and such money as there was
used for buying more insurance

years ago it came to me
how cold his white feet must have been
in the new shoes shined perfectly
to step out where the ice was thin
mind made up against drink and sin
smoking swearing cards and dancing
the bad boys who liked playing in
streets and the threat in everything

and then a big church of his own
when he had never finished school
that looming Presbyterian
flawed yellow brick tabernacle
that they told him used to be full
behind it passers-by could see
across the river to the still
skyline of the shining city

on the eve of the Depression
there he stayed marking time for years
before he turned and started down
through latter-day architectures
largely maintained by faith and prayers
pinched salaries lame in coming
decades later he said in tears
that he had failed at everything

but I had seen him with the old
the sick and dying and alone
sometimes all they may need he told
me one time is to have someone
listen to them and he had known
by then the voices growing small
the smells of beds the waiting bone
the pictures far off on the wall

and screams out of the wells of pain
shaking the curtains in the night
the breath starting its climb again
the eyes rolling away in fright
liquids glittering through the light
colors opening on the bed
the hands still hoping as the white
shadows tightened around the head

Aunt Sue so shrunk inside her skin
that toward the last they could not find
a vein to put a needle in
he had heard what they had in mind
as they lay staring at the end
it was still something he was told
he prayed with them and he was kind
and then he wanted to be old

helpless and taken care of by
somebody else he always said
he had something wrong with him they
had never found though they had tried
until the night one sat beside
him reading psalms and as he read
Therefore will not we fear he died
saying that he was not afraid

which I do hope and trust was so
a thing to save and put away
by then maybe they did not know
and surely neither one could say
what had stayed with them all the way
apart from any names for it
three times she bowed her head to say
good-night to the closing casket

alone then as she chose to be
she set her own house in order
even neater than formerly
from the glassed back porch table where
she had her meals and opened her
mail she looked out on the garden
and the rain of that cold summer
not good weather to be out in

she wrote her letters there when she
had washed and dried the dishes her
dread as she put it was to be
a burden to someone ever
not to be able to take care
of herself eventually
that was one thing she had never
wished to live long enough to see

she had examples close to hand
the old friends whom she visited
who could no longer understand
her name or anything she said
but stared up at her from the bed
when they recognized in her place
someone she knew had long been dead
she felt a cloud across her face

then nursing homes and hospitals
walkers and wheel chairs and IV's
letters with medical details
tolling losses of faculties
tumors and incapacities
strokes attacks vistas of the ward
and the vacant paralysis
no one could alter or afford

friends wrote of places she might go
communities planned for the old
she sat writing by the window
while the gray days went on she told
how high the weeds had grown this cold
had made the berries late again
and to pick them she had to hold
the big umbrella in the rain

and yet she had no wish to move
the winter was the only thing
that worried her she would not leave
her neighbor who came that evening
when her number went on ringing
had trouble opening the door
tripped over the body lying
where it had been left just before

when I am gone she used to say
get the Salvation Army in
have them take everything away
but when the time came I moved in
turned in rooms where their lives had been
and emptied out cupboards and shelves
drawers cabinets cellar kitchen
of things not worth much in themselves

then all at once it was autumn
the leaves turning and the light clear
and I was watching the day come
into the branches floating near
the window where year after year
I woke up looking into them
shots in the woods told of a deer
somewhere and crows called after them

my parents gone I met their friends
over again someone each day
gave them whatever odds and ends
they were inclined to take away
listened to what they had to say
of what appealed to them and why
cut glass or dolls or dinner tray
lives were to be remembered by

clothes went to be passed on to some
murmured names whom I never knew
after most of those who had come
whose sayings I had listened to
I was left wordless with a new
rear-view figure I had been shown
another aspect of those two
whom I was certain I had known

my brother-in-law finally
came with a rental van one day
my sister and her family
carried the furniture away
we stood outside trying to say
what might remain still to be said
then they got going all the way
to Michigan taking the bed

I stayed there among the echoes
planning to finish up a few
last things a clear day toward the close
of autumn I still had to do
one the instructions urged me to
Burn these it said in my mother's
hand on the bundle and I knew
who had written her those letters

and all of my father's sermons
his note consigned now to the fire
even the one in which I once
in childhood had heard him inquire
What have we lost and listened for
the answer but was never sure
it would be somewhere in the pyre
and would escape me as before

I took them out into the garden
past the fence to the iron drum
they had kept there to burn things in
lit the first page saw the flame climb
into the others fed it some
later years and then the letters
set the grill safely over them
as the fire rose to burn for hours

morning flowed over the bare floor
after everything had been done
nothing was left to come back for
I could not tell then what had gone
or whether or all of us had known
that daylight in the empty room
that I had not seen until then
that had no story and no name

I had given those things away
that never had belonged to me
and by that time whose life were they
whose ornaments and memory
even those days that seemed to be
mine went off somewhere on their own
disappearing in front of me
before I saw that they were gone

years earlier when I was young
I sat up with Old French to read
Villon in his unbroken tongue
knowing by then that I would need
his own words if I was indeed
to hear what their rough accent tells
playing across a kind of deed
that left things to somebody else

his voice gone from it long ago
a shadow on an empty lake
those names drifting through its echo
pronounced now only for the sake
of the turns he contrived to make
at their expense who in their time
sat on everything they could take
and let the rest gaze up at them

and they had blown away in dust
and the gross volumes of their fame
had shrunk to footnotes at the last
which the readers of a poem
looked up only because some name
had stopped them in a passage there
but that was not what they had come
to be reading the poem for

even the language of their day
had grown foreign not just to me
no one had spoken it that way
lo this many a century
some of those words remained only
because his pen had set them down
one night before he was thirty
as the bell tolled at the Sorbonne

hard as it was to catch the wave
of song running those syllables
from a voice in an unknown grave
that could have been nobody else
a note out of the ground that calls
unaltered from the start I heard
and its own moment without bells
that went on ringing afterward

I walked out in the summer night
under the silent canopy
of sycamores along the street
and his words made it seem to me
how easy in his century
writing a poem must have been
I was some years short of twenty
and saw the ease was plain Villon

cat burglar's ninth life wanted for
assorted acts of robbery
including churches also for
murder caught tortured ripe to die
freed in a round of amnesty
to his underworld haunts and whores
used up gone missing at thirty
with no suggestion of remorse

who could believe a thing he said
though he swore on one testicle
that it was love alone that had
brought him to this deplorable
state and to drawing up his will
in verse giving it all away
which was more true than probable
like someone dying in a play

at twenty what first stayed with me
were his long slow notes and the snows
then in a few years I would be
the age he was when he wrote those
first parting words while the ink froze
that was youth of which he would say
so soon how suddenly it goes
and all at once has flown away

no one would write that way again
forever after as I knew
but in a dream that I had then
more than once I climbed up into
the attic and went over to
that trunk forbidden as the Ark
which no eye ever looked into
under the rafters in the dark

once when my father opened it
he said how long it had been since
those boots went hunting coon at night
and when my mother looked in once
she unwrapped a dress and ribbons
laughing at what had come to light
garments and relics of her parents
ghostly gloves and lace veils still white

when I opened it in the dream
besides what I remembered there
I found hidden along with them
bundles of writing paper where
poems I had forgotten were
formed in a hand that was my own
as I read they seemed familiar
and they all sounded like Villon

and there I left them as I thought
but then as I was coming near
the rapids and had almost shot
into my own thirtieth year
I thought I should set down before
its end a farewell reckoning
of what was bound to disappear
with that youth which I was leaving

and with the clock face looking on
I wrote out a few notes in some
manner that seemed right to me then
but finding how far I was from
settling yet with the time to come
put the half-hearted things away
where I might get to them some time
possibly on a later day

and now already it is May
one of these nights the plovers flew
north they had vanished on their way
when the stars rose that told them to
and it was days before we knew
while they had reached the northern lights
and white days and were coming to
where first they rose into their flights

and in our turn we felt the roar
loose us once more down the runway
and we were flung far out before
ourselves lifting above the day
the coast of shadows fell away
a time of clouds walking in sleep
carried us on its turning way
another light crossing the deep

into a late age sinking toward
that gray light where the ghosts go home
a time before long afterward
its halls through which the echoes come
with their sounds trailing after them
swirling down the shadowy air
then the way south another time
resurfaced but still going there

turn after turn appearing as
leaves floating just under water
each the newest in a series
and at evening arriving here
at the ridge above the river
garden and house in the long light
that fades from them as we appear
in time to see them before night

all of their seasons shut away
the garden not remembering
but the hand older in the way
the key turns in the opening
smell of wood and the house waking
here and there out of its shadows
through the blackbird's evening warning
from the trees under the windows

naming the twilight from before
with the first stars there already
and from outside the terrace door
over the village roofs we see
this year the comet steadily
lighting the sky it has come through
while points kindle in the valley
the constellation Bretenoux

the dark comes slowly in late spring
still cold in the first nights of May
I woke through it imagining
the bright path of a single ray
from that house we left far away
then I remembered where we were
and those were lights down on the way
that we had taken to come here

later the singing wakened me
those long notes again beginning
out of the dark crown of a tree
in the oak wood their slow rising
tumbling down into a rushing
stream while from farther along
the ridge another listening
nightingale begins its own song

under this roof I listened to
the singing of their ancestors
forbears these voices never knew
now it is more than forty years
since I first peered through the shutters
into an empty house along
wrecked walls and rubble on the floors
where no one had lived for that long

and almost that long since the night
I first set up the folding bed
carried in through the evening light
while the swallows brushed past my head
to the beams where they had nested
it was this season and I heard
later the sounds the dark house made
and then that singing afterward

I slept into another time
and the sayings of a country
that before summer had become
more recognizable to me
than strands of my own memory
though it was not where I was from
and my own words would never be
the common speech where I had come

I could believe only in part
what my own days had led me to
belonging elsewhere from the start
or so I thought *I expect you*
had not wanted the garden too
he said before he signed the deed
I answered at once that I knew
it was the garden I would need

Mentiére's potatoes for one year
then digging through the overgrown
docks and nettles in late autumn
to put a patch of lettuce in
and turning up bits of iron
broken forks square nails made by hand
cow shoes shell buttons that had been
gone for a long time in that ground

then hearing when the trees were still
naked in spring some cold morning
the garden door scrape on its sill
and it was old Delsol coming
with the cows and again threading
them through the doorway one by one
to plow the garden following
his voice as they had always done

his voice reaching back to them then
seems to come from no farther now
than when their breaths were braided in
the rows and as they turned the plow
rose over the finished furrow
then the bowed heads came back again
to where I watch until they go
out through the door above the lane

sound of that door crossing the stone
words calling to silent creatures
close behind that is the garden
that has vanished and reappears
surfacing behind the others
as the new leaves and loved faces
unfold out of a fan of years
and it lives among their shadows

and if ever I am to make
a rough draft of a reckoning
along the lines it was to take
at the moment youth was heading
out into the darkness flying
toward its own north and to this day
the one place that it was going
so far to find no one can say

I suppose I could start it here
at the house that one time I knew
maybe as well as anywhere
it was in youth that I came to
that door and by now there are few
ways left into those painted caves
that a light might still wander through
and find footprints of former lives

though indeed I have never known
much of note about those who were
here in the days before my own
met one woman who was born here
but whatever I might ask her
she had little enough to tell
of what she had left behind her
when she married out of it all

I wonder through what window she
first saw that time and from what room
and where the beds were in which they
woke and died and now not a name
remains from any family
then there were nuns who taught school here
at the turn of the century
in the years growing toward the war

only what now is left to me
can I hope to guide as it goes
looking north over the valley
from this room where the oven is
that baked their bread in the old days
for this place I too left behind
often and in so many ways
and set the feather in the wind

in deadly half-earnest Villon
launching into a legacy
found before he had well begun
that the form allowed him every
kind of digression and delay
that would put off the bitter list
which I confess appeals to me
who would rather leave that for last

my life was never so precious
to me as now James Wright once wrote
and then looked at his words and was
he said taken aback by what
he saw there but some thought like that
lives in my mind these years these days
through which the speed that is the light
brings me to see it as it goes

a bright cloud on a spring morning
lit with more than I remember
the first rays of sunrise turning
from the ridge across the river
along the valley and over
the young leaves and Paula waking
and I am still on the way here
seeing long before believing

how can this be the moment for
pointing all of it on its way
and putting out next to the door
those parting words that never say
much of what they were meant to say
although I know it would be wise
since none of this has long to stay
to learn to kiss it as it flies

and try to put in order some
provision or at least pretense
of that and with good grace in time
in spite of the way documents
have of making another sense
quite unforeseen when they were signed
to suit a later circumstance
and the bent of a different mind

did Villon's heirs ever collect
anything that he meant for them
yet in fact what could he expect
when some items he left for them
varied in quality and some
were not registered in his name
and never had belonged to him
which would have made them hard to claim

but when it comes to that there are
things that I take to be my own
that I would like a good home for
and would be happy to pass on
only I see I do not own
even the present worth of them
for numbering and handing down
so nothing will be lost of them

and though whatever I may leave
is clear to me how can I say
what an heir will in fact receive
when even now the words I say
sometimes are heard another way
as nothing is dependable
while I still have the chance I may
as well bestow things as I will

I leave to Paula this late spring
with its evenings in the garden
all the years of it beginning
from the moment I met her in
Fran's living room and the veiled green
leaves were young that we walked under
that night it was still April then
as we started home together

and to Paula besides the rest
that my mother called tangibles
whatever singing I have missed
from the darkness beyond the walls
the long notes of those nightingales
that began before I listened
first to their unrepeated calls
that song that never seems to end

and wakes the wren in the deep night
and the blackbird before morning
as we lie watching the moonlight
that has remembered everything
the stones of the old house shining
the cloud of light veiling the hill
and the river below shining
upwards as though it were still

there will be other things of course
as with Paula there always are
early light seen from later years
every vanishing reminder
of the way our days together
suddenly are there behind us
ours still but somewhere else before
we believed they were leaving us

or understood how they could go
like that faster than we can see
in spite of everything we know
and would have done to make them stay
they were already on their way
and their speed quickened when we came
to meet and there ignorantly
began these years in love with time

this year when the wild strawberries
only now begin to ripen
along the wall above the house
as I set foot in the garden
early this morning from my own
shadow there floats up as lightly
as the shadow if it had flown
a black redstart there before me

alighting a few feet away
the rust tail feathers quivering
as weightless as its flight the way
a hand trembles above a string
and the eye a black pearl holding
me and the new daylight on each
leaf around us in the morning
in that moment just out of reach

where I stood in other seasons
in the same garden long ago
and heard the clack of those small stones
under water letting me know
that a forbear of this shadow
with the same song and charactery
but far from either of us now
was nearby with an eye on me

and down the long rows of those days
observed what I was doing then
from the house roof or young pear trees
diving and appearing again
on the fork I left standing in
the ground out there and turned away
a moment the bird was there when
I turned back as it is today

as close as once it would appear
to those who in their time have stood
on this ground before I was here
that song was here before they made
their way up into the oak wood
and first herded stones around them
there was always something they did
that made this shadow follow them

and something that I came to do
later that it would recognize
at once and keep returning to
taking me each time by surprise
though how I figured in its eyes
I cannot say but as one who
brought the dark up to the surface
showing this ancient what was new

some would never heed anything
so small and as they thought of no
use to them but some kept finding
names for how it came to follow
and would vanish in the furrow
turning up just in front of them
and gone before they saw it go
a trick of shadow on a stream

coming so close and never held
seeming to have no weight at all
a pausing flourish whose wings fold
black as a cloak above the tail
that color that will not be still
which I have seen in the first light
fade out and return after all
with the sun setting into it

what could we know of each other
by the light of the same morning
in the moment that we were there
I could see that its mate was waiting
in a bush nearby repeating
those fine notes over and over
which the first one was echoing
something like I am here I am here

I leave what makes them reappear
out of my shadow once again
in a May morning of this year
and what in me they may have seen
without more fright than they have shown
and safe distance and whatever
between us never will be known
to them and to their heirs forever

and I leave to Jannah Arnoux
on this day when she turns eighty
the old house that she came back to
all those years out of each city
affair or eminence that she
had managed or been brought to in
the long story of her beauty
where she always began again

since the first day that she stared in
across the sill as a strange child
too small for school and old women
kissed her face that had just travelled
from the other side of the world
which she had seen sink in the sea
Indochina then it was called
they said they were her family

unlike the others she had lost
the Chinese mother scarcely known
French father whose brother a priest
could not bring her up on his own
so sent her home and would have gone
himself if only God had willed
all of them shrank and darkened then
in the memory of a child

who grew up to the haute couture
one black braid almost to the floor
for Ricci then the Prefecture
as the wife smiling at the door
to diplomats before the war
then a cell in the Resistance
the Gestapo were dying for
on a side street in Vichy France

still in her twenties when the bells
kept ringing that the war was done
with its fathomless burials
and still looking no older than
when first she stepped down from that train
to Paris and her student days
she turned toward the turns of fashion
a shrewdness she claimed was Chinese

years in the capital and yet
all of her youth seemed still with her
in full assurance when she met
Serge painting frescoes in a bar
and they started designing their
fabric that reached from an antique
house in a nearby market square
Paris Corsica Martinique

stores and houses in all of them
seasons spent in far-off places
this was still where they lived and came
in at the door of the same house
and heard the rooms hear their voices
as though they never had been gone
they keep planning to leave it less
they agree as the years go on

I leave her all the orchards on
the south hill and the road climbing
up through the tilled vineyards of Glanes
with the peach blossoms opening
and the moments of homecoming
grown into one to reappear
as it seemed something was being
given back in the spring this year

and to Serge good and gentle friend
painter musician cook so graced
with talents that some have opened
all by themselves and run to waste
gardener startled by how fast
even the long summer twilight
starts to go and straightens at last
to gaze out on the rest of it

I leave the tiered ridges beyond
Cornac with the mist deepening
in the valleys and the darkened
grapes across the bronze slope waiting
with the autumn light ripening
the time of harvest like a pear
then the hushed snow he loves along
the terraces of Quarante Peires

beyond the far end of the year
and I leave to Fernande Delsol
while the spring is still with us here
that echoes from outside the wall
the clack of her hoe in the cool
morning before the dew is dry
with her grandchildren off to school
and her kitchen standing empty

and her hat above the row
of young green at that hour casting
on the ancient wall its shadow
her back clenched from years of lying
awake coughing scarcely breathing
one daughter dead the other gone
saying now she is profiting
while the day has not yet begun

what can I leave her after all
that I know would give her pleasure
when it was always hard to tell
what would be right to bring to her
if it was something she might wear
with her plain tastes anything too
obvious would embarrass her
shy as she is of what is new

and never one for wasting time
wishing for things that were not hers
though I hear her from time to time
wish for health hers or another's
and for rain in the dry summers
and for the grandchildren to stay
out of trouble a few more years
and then get married properly

and wish for coming days to be
spared evils that still lie in wait
and I nod each time and agree
wishing kind health weather and fate
upon us both and beyond that
though it is hazardous to give
somebody else a present that
the one who gives would like to have

leave her the morning as it is
clear and still with the bell from down
across the valley reaching us
to say the hour over again
so that we can pay attention
to what time it may be this time
looking up at the one between
the ones told and the next to come

and seeing what was always there
the furrows traced across the field
in the same places where they were
when she looked at them as a child
the new leaves glowing on the old
trees in the time before her eyes
and a day she had not beheld
until then take her by surprise

I leave the house itself again
and close the door remembering
Ruhe sanft mein holdes Leben
heard on another day in spring
the shimmer of those notes floating
through the open door years ago
some of them are still echoing
through us northward as we go

down from the ridge under the high
cries of kites wheeling while the sun
climbs past them into the clear sky
all the wheels are turning by then
too fast to see and we fly on
and as the lights come on return
across the humming bridge again
to the nova where I was born

and evening on Washington Square
Margaret home her door opening
and John and Aleksandra there
dinner all together talking
over last plans for their wedding
guests flowers music clothes with less
than two days to spend rehearsing
the program and its promises

besides that to be practical
I leave them now for future use
something that both of them know well
the long light on the avenues
Fifth or Seventh or they may choose
when the moment occurs to them
early or late a day like this
in spring or a day in autumn

and I leave Matthew and Karen
who flew in from San Francisco
on the eve of this occasion
carrying Luke the baby to
the wedding with months still to go
before his first light year has flown
I leave a message for him now
for them to give him later on

and for themselves to take back west
flashes from another island
signalling farther up the coast
the salt wind racing from beyond
the whetted shadow where the land
vanishes under the wide glare
summer and its lingering sound
through the days they remember there

as others do who have for years
returned there thanks to Margaret
her auspices in what is hers
that whole shoreline of Nantucket
that she sees as first she saw it
a Coast Guard station on the dune
where an age put out the whaleboat
praying they would get back again

hers and for her also remain
the fresh snow outside the windows
when she has stayed to read alone
and the moment the fox passes
and she does not know what he sees
while the winter sun flashes on
the wings of swans gathered across
the long pond at Little Compton

I wake now in her house again
in that part of the galaxy
where my view of this round began
in the stone cloud in the city
and the sparks flying around me
were the moments of all the days
that I had come so far to see
some of them I would recognize

and some I thought burned a long time
in the same section of the sky
and my way came so close to them
they were the worlds that I saw by
so when their light was gone if I
closed my eyes there appeared to be
a day still present in the eye
that made the dark harder to see

the Manhattan for which I had
no name the moment I was born
bit after bit had orbited
into place and was being torn
down and I would see it return
as glittering reflections cast
in clusters high adrift in turn
through their towers of blowing dust

so that already it was late
when first it burned before my eyes
and they opened into the light
and gazed out upon a surface
where features without faces rose
revolved and went away again
that was the only way it was
and the way it had always been

it turned out that the world was old
I stood up to see it was so
all the stories that I was told
happened such a long time ago
there was nobody left to know
at what time they had once been true
and after that where did they go
only my hearing them was new

and the light as it came to me
and for a moment was the day
in appearance was new to me
though it had travelled a long way
the whole night had fallen away
behind it since it had begun
that sole occurence of its way
through the dark before anyone

the city moving on the screen
now is the latest in a line
and the others that I have seen
here in the years that have been mine
turning into each other shine
through the fresh colors everywhere
and I see where I am again
knowing what is no longer there

that age just beneath the surface
where I lived at the high windows
north and east on Waverly Place
and woke to watch as the sun rose
over the stacks and roofs across
the Village and all day and night
the long mirrors the panes of glass
the walls wheeled with the passing light

before I left for anywhere
even if it was not for long
I climbed the last stairs to the door
onto the roof and turned among
the compass points to look along
the dark line across the river
where at one time when I was young
I tried to see what might be here

as the cars on the avenue
rushed in one current under me
red lights bobbing on their way to
the tunnel I hoped I would be
back before long to that city
and find everything still the same
as I was leaving it and we
would wake up there in the next time

how did it vanish even as
I stood watching at the window
I heard after dark the horses
at eleven when they would go
passing in double file below
the trembling panes and take the day
under all its blue helmets to
the barn down there a little way

when they had passed I thought I heard
a hush follow them for a while
in the avenue afterward
lasting perhaps only until
the lights changed by the hospital
and the late taxis thinning out
at that hour lunged ahead to sail
their double tracers down the street

and as the days themselves have gone
friends have not been there suddenly
so many leaving one by one
each of them taking a city
we knew that will not again be
seen until last night's barn gives back
once more into the coming day
the sons of laughing Gruagach

so many gone and there it burns
the stone flames climbing as they did
flashing again while the day turns
colors not caught or recorded
not recalled never repeated
fire of this time my one city
of what the light remembers made
bright present turn to ash slowly

now there remain out of those days
fewer friends than there used to be
there is more left than we can use
of this still unfinished city
running its old film Mercury
poised at corners over the pulse
that pounds as the living hurry
already late for somewhere else

as a child I came on a bridge
we rose over the white river
I saw all down the farther edge
shadows standing by the water
shining one behind another
the cables ran past one by one
then there were none and we were there
but the place I had seen was gone

in time I learned they were the same
though I could not say what they are
out of which these scant heirlooms come
that I must set in order for
friends still residing here and there
between the rivers though it is
a while since I have noted their
true condition in some cases

to Mike Keeley since I believe
we have been friends since both of us
were beginning to shave I leave
for his free uncontested use
what stretch of Morton Street may please
him best and his own choice of neighbors
and a magic wand to ease
his vacuum cleaner up the stairs

and for his guests who come to town
his own family or Mary's
or Jacqueline and Clarence Brown
I leave him the old Getty place
to remind them a bit of Greece
those white though flaking capitals
that facade out of other days
the severe lines of the old walls

Getty I suspect had not stayed
there for some time and it may be
no one after him had loved it
so the great plantations empty
and with the house naturally
goes the walled ailanthus garden
behind it for Mike and Mary
on spring evenings to wander in

and I leave to Galway Kinnell
friend I think for about as long
since those days in the dining hall
as waiters when we were too young
for the war and later coming
from Europe after years away
meeting again half believing
to compare notes in the city

the whole of Greenwich Street that runs
along the Hudson where the piers
stagger and groan when the tide turns
complaining idly by the waters
their tones drowned by the truck motors
tires on cobbles shouts unloading
carcasses into warehouse doors
and the racks of iron ringing

I leave him in particular
out of the high wall of facades
that look west across the river
toward Jersey and the Palisades
one where the wooden staircase leads
above a sausage factory
redolent echoing splintered treads
reaching the top floor finally

dusty machines and black pulleys
in the ceiling and a transom
ajar over the door that was
the way the burglar must have come
as he saw once when he got home
but had not taken anything
I hope he finds it all this time
just the same with nothing missing

to Jay Laughlin so he will have
somewhere to lay his head when he
stays in the city now I leave
at the west end of Waverly
on Bank Street the brick house where he
once learned the true height of the doors
so that wherever he may be
he knows it after all these years

and I leave to James Baker Hall
circling as the white pigeons do
above those roofs as though he still
were attached to a loft he knew
up over Seventh Avenue
his feet again in that high place
and for his coming to and fro
by the blue door his parking space

I leave Ben Sonnenberg the whole
of Eighth Street west of Fifth although
the fire keeps taking such a toll
it is scarcely the Rialto
that I expect he used to know
parts of a different parade
show up for dress rehearsals now
guessing what games are being played

to Richard Howard who has been
a perpetual prodigy
from the first phoneme he took in
I leave that end of Waverly
above the university
where the Villages east and west
echo each other endlessly
below the books that line his nest

and at moments to come when he
turns from words or from whatever
art sense discourse or faculty
held his attention I leave for
him to glance up and recover
the flash of that late salmon light
before sunset off the river
that glows along Eleventh Street

and to his gentle neighbor Grace
Schulman at that corner they share
already where Waverly Place
runs west into Washington Square
musicians jugglers the street fair
the sounds of an invisible
river rushing around her there
that she hears now when she stands still

to Bill Matthews to hear again
every note as he pleases though
he seems at home now far uptown
I leave the music that for so
long rose from under my window
that Vanguard where a few of his
late heroes used to come and go
with the sun in the black cases

to Harry Ford so he will have
somewhere disposed to keep body
and soul agreeable I leave
at the moment the Gramercy
Tavern and Union Square Café
both for variety an art
demands devotion constantly
though the taste of it may be short

to Alastair Reid born nomad
child of one island moving on
island by island satisfied
with what he could pack neatly in
a suitcase I leave on this stone
as it changes in the water
all the islands that he has known
turning up out of each other

to Francesco Pellizzi for
wherever he wants it to be
I leave the stillness of the water
toward the end of a winter day
at South Street by the Battery
the rivers gathered into one
that turns the color of the sky
and the lights starting to come on

I leave Gerald Stern the window
into his old apartment on
106th Street although
just the outside looking in
to see himself as he was then
and the faces still there in stone
before the five flights on Van Dam
and the windows that gaze uptown

over the low roofs toward that gray
tower cut out of another
plane part shadow making the day
in whose sky it appears appear
hard to believe shaped of mid-air
a specter named for some remote
image of another empire
that high beams color now at night

I stood beside that building one
summer before I started school
my mother took me that time when
she was getting me dressed for fall
we took the ferry to Canal
in those days and the street cars had
the sides open to keep them cool
a breeze came to us as we rode

the escalators of that day
Macy's I think and probably
Best's bird cages she used to say
that she never liked that city
but there were times it seemed when she
was happy to be there standing
beside a fountain telling me
who that was in gold and flying

we were walking down Lexington
and she said we were going to
pass the highest building in
the world the one she said I knew
that we always looked over to
across the river but today
I would stand and be able to
see up to the top all the way

after I had done that she said
if I would think of all that height
as the time the earth existed
before life had begun on it
yes with the spire on top of it
and the lightning rod then the time
since life began would lie on that
like a book she read to us from

and the whole age when there had been
life of the kind we knew which we
came to call human and our own
on top of that closed book would be
to the time underneath it only
as thick as one stamp that might be
on a post card but we would see
none of that where we were today

we walked along the avenue
over the stamp I had not seen
where would the card be going to
that the stamp was to be put on
would I see what was written down
on it whenever it was sent
and the few words what would they mean
that we took with us as we went

INAUGURATION

Whose was the hand then
around the bolted door
that first night in the house
empty for decades
beyond the dark floor piled with rubble
while outside the broken panes only the long
unseen cold grass of spring was stirring

one hand like a gray rag fluttering
unmistakable in the black doorway
inching toward the bolt as though
a wind were pushing it from behind
and a dim light going before it
leading this way this way

the swallows in the beams
never stirred in their own furled sleep
no sound came from the cracks in the walls
Even if it went away
I would have seen it
even if it did nothing
it would know I had come

A CLAIM

Even through the days as a believer
doubt would shadow the distant light
over the valley deep in itself
the voices that rang clear of it
never lingered
and long before I left
I had already gone

each time I turned away
it all stepped into that water
where it would seem to be the same
almost the same
and the heart would sink at the sight of it
without knowing why
the same heart come again
once more expecting nothing
and caught by what was never there

THAT MUSIC

By the time I came to hear about it
I was assured that there was no such thing
no it was one more in the long trailing
troupe of figures that had been believed but
had never existed no it had not
resounded in the dark at the beginning
no among the stars there was no singing
then or later no ringing single note
threaded the great absences no echoing
of space in space no there was no calling
along the lights anywhere no it was not
in the choiring of water in the saying
of a name it was not living or warning
through the thrush of dusk or the wren of morning

THE WREN

Paper clips are rusted to the pages
before I have come back to hear a bell
I recognize out of another age
echo from the cold mist of one morning
in white May and then a wren still singing
from the thicket at the foot of the wall

that is one of the voices without question
and without answer like the beam of some
star familiar but in no sense known threading
time upon time on its solitary way
once more I hear it without understanding
and without division in the new day

SYLLABLES

Mornings of fog with the voices of birds
flicking through it names rising to whisper
after them like the mist closing behind
I have brought my life here where it must have been once
whitethroat chaffinch who see everything once
I have brought it back remembering them
so there must be something of it here now
in the fog flying once without a name

WANTING TO SEE

Some moss might be the color of the book
in which all the feathers were black and white
it was better that way they assured her
turning the pages never trust colors
of birds on paper in life they are not
like that the true ones flying in a day
that has since been removed they have been seen
looking out through their names in those black trees
the river turned white before you were born

ORIOLES

The song of the oriole began as an echo
but this year it was not heard afterward
or before or at all and only later
would anyone notice what had not been there
when the cuckoo had been heard again
a calling shadow but not the goldfinch
with its gold and not that voice through the waterfall
the oriole flashing under the window
among the trees now at the end of the hall
of the palace one of the palaces
St Augustine told about Here he said
you enter into the great palaces
of memory and whose palaces were they
I wondered at first knowing that he
must have been speaking from memory
of his own of palaces of his own
with his own days echoing in the halls

JEANNE DUVAL

There are those he said
who would not be at all surprised
that it seemed to you
familiar as you have named it
though remember that
we who have been here all the time
seeing it as our
own are less likely to have it
emerge before us
for the first time ancient as light
and know it at once
out of all we have forgotten

now that you tell us
how it appeared to you he said
we catch sight of it
ourselves as you may have seen it
in this deep forest
the valley curtained with shadows
of oaks the mossed roofs
where the tracks come out of the woods
the hamlet of Jeanne
Duval and rising from the lane
this one plain building
its pink stone glowing like a lamp

arches at the base
of the walls none like the others
across wide porches
opened at different times into
the main manor of
Jeanne Duval perhaps it was this
which you thought you were
seeing years ago beside those
oaks and that fountain
that empty village those arches
that tower and one
old man trying to remember

it would not be true
to say we knew you were coming
any more than we
can think that the ancestors knew
that we would be here
but just as your sight of the house
the sound of its name
from the line of mothers the door
where you came into
the swirl of dogs children faces
of different ages
to stand in a large family

set your blood beating
suddenly faster as though you
had been there before
so each of us seems to know you
and will tell you that
after you have gone in to meet
Jeanne Duval herself
she will be happy to see you
how long it has been
some of it will come back something
that you recognize
you will know her when you see her

SHEEP PASSING

Mayflies hover through the long evening
of their light and in the winding lane
the stream of sheep runs among shadows calling
the old throats gargling again uphill
along known places once more and from the bells
borne by their predecessors the notes
dull as wood clonk to the flutter of all
the small hooves over the worn stone
with the voices of the lambs rising through them
over and over telling and asking
their one question into the day they have
none will know midsummer the walls of the lane
are older than anyone can understand
and the lane must have been a path a long time
before the first stones were raised beside it
and must have been a trail from the river
up through the trees for an age before that
one hoof one paw one foot before another
the way they went is all that is still there

MOISSAC

Now I see it after years of holding
reflections of parts of it in my mind
children have been born here and have grown up
married gone off to war divorced and died
since the last time I stood on these same stones
whose white is the color I remember
but I see the colors of all of them
on walls and here and there on the carved stones
had fallen away from me as they had
been falling before I had ever seen them
from the walls and the figures carved in stone
it is quieter than I remember
smaller of course and closer and the smile
of Eve harder than ever to see there
is it a smile after all the hollow
in the stone face by the doorway looking
down at the serpent climbing onto her
in silence neither one hearing ages
behind them from which they have come nor those
before them in the colors of the days

SEED TIME

The old photographs the prints that survived
made their way into the days of August
into the backs of the deep glaring noons
August came and already they were in place
old in arrival and knowing the ways
of settlers though not of the first ones they
recall no colors nor what those were good for
initials have become dust and shadows
water is wrapped in sheets and glass is blank
but here and there faces go on staring
from paper without moving or noticing
that August has come that this is August
here is the bird of August and the dry breeze
stirring the leaves in the dust of morning
here is the white sky that has come at last
here is the bright day the prints have led to

FRAME

But look this is not yet
the other age
this is the only one
between the brown
pictures and the blank film

there was even
a sign saying Today
in a window
but what it was announcing
was days ago

I forget now
what it was there to say
it was something
else whatever
is announced is over

whether or not
it has been seen at dusk
when it is time
to grow up and too late
to take pictures

SHORE BIRDS

While I think of them they are growing rare
after the distances they have followed
all the way to the end for the first time
tracing a memory they did not have
until they set out to remember it
at an hour when all at once it was late
and newly silent and the white had turned
white around them then they rose in their choir
on a single note each of them alone
between the pull of the moon and the hummed
undertone of the earth below them
the glass curtains kept falling around them
as they flew in search of their place before
they were anywhere and storms winnowed them
they flew among the places with towers
and passed the tower lights where some vanished
with their long legs for wading in shadow
others were caught and stayed in the countries
of the nets and in the lands of the lime twigs
some fastened and after the countries of
guns at first light fewer of them than I
remember would be here to recognize
the light of late summer when they found it
playing with darkness along the wet sand

WAVES IN AUGUST

There is a war in the distance
with the distance growing smaller
the field glasses lying at hand
are for keeping it far away

I thought I was getting better
about that returning childish
wish to be living somewhere else
that I knew was impossible
and now I find myself wishing
to be here to be alive here
it is impossible enough
to still be the wish of a child

in youth I hid a boat under
the bushes beside the water
knowing I would want it later
and come back and would find it there
someone else took it and left me
instead the sound of the water
with its whisper of vertigo

terror reassurance an old
old sadness it would seem we knew
enough always about parting
but we have to go on learning
as long as there is anything

TRAVELLING WEST AT NIGHT

I remember waking at the rivers
to see girders of gray sleepless bridges
appearing from sleep out of a current
of cold night air velvet with the secret
coal smoke of those small hours and nobody
on night roads the few words of toll-keepers
old complaints of gates and cables the bark
of bridge floors leaping up from under us
and the swelling hiss of a surface just
beneath us not loud but while it was there
nothing else could be heard except as calls
far off in some distance meaning that we
were already there in the dark country
before in the land beyond the rivers
one by one past the clutched hunches of sleep
the black country where we were expected
was waiting ahead of us on the far
shore unchanged remembering us even
when we had forgotten and then we went
on into the wordless dark beyond each
river thinking that we were going back

THIS TIME

Many things I seem to have done backward
as a child I wanted to be older
now I am trying to remember why
and what it was like to have to pretend
day after day I saw places that I
did not recognize until later on
when nothing was left of them any more
there were meetings and partings that passed me
at the time like train windows with the days
slipping across them and long afterward
the moment and sense of them came to me
burning there were faces I knew for years
and the nearness of them began only
when they were missing and there were seasons
of anguish I recalled with affection
joys lost unnoticed and searched for later
with no sign to show where they had last been
there with me and there was love which is thought
to be a thing of youth and I found it
I was sure that was what it was as I
came to it again and again sometimes
without knowing it sometimes insisting
vainly upon the name but I came to
the best of it last and though it may be
shorter this way I am glad it is so
it would have been too brief at any time
and so much of what I had found early
had been lost as I made my way to this
which is what I was to know afterward

THE NOTES

I was not the right age to begin
to be taught to play the violin
Dr Perpetuo told my father
when I was four with these very hands
were we too young in his opinion
or were we already too old by then
I come now with no real preparation
to finger the extinct instruments
that I know only by reputation
after these years of trying to listen
to learn what I was listening for
what it is that I am trying to hear
it is something I had begun
giving ear to all unknown
before that day with its explanation
about the strings and how before you can
play the notes you have to make each one
I never even learned how to listen

LEFT HAND

One morning I look at it with surprise
that gives off a known but fathomless sound
what is it that I recognize with such
unappeased gratitude this is what I
have taken to be my own all my life
my own left hand that had nothing to do
but what I wanted as well as it could
that grew up with me as a part of me
with no mind of its own that I know of
and no existence apart from my own
its scars its habits are my own story
it does not hear what I say about it
or know what I know of its long journey
before it was mine the little finger
reaching to touch the thumb the first time
startled speechless finding the way to it
again kindling a brightness beyond it
to which it belonged and with which it was
going what can I say to it even
now when it has helped me on to the words
that have been picked up before I had learned
what they might be for and when the time comes
to use them what can they hold and carry
how far can they reach what sense will they touch

LATE GLIMPSE

They were years younger than I am
centuries ago
when they spoke of themselves as old
looking at the empty sky

end of November as we call it now
winter light no age over the gray sea
a petrel flies in at evening
trailing its feet in the sunset

ACCOMPANIMENT

Day alone first of December with rain
falling lightly again in the garden
and the dogs sleeping on the dark floorboards
day between journeys unpacking from one

then packing for another and reading
poems as I go words from a time past
light migrants coming from so long ago
through the sound of this quiet rain falling

FIELD NOTE

Its marbled fields remember spring
dew in the bare light shimmering
and the surprise of beginning
when there was only the morning
with its unknown high clouds passing
neither pausing nor listening
while its branches were opening
white flowers to their day shining
that one time and a bell ringing
in the north and no one counting

THE STRING

Night the black bead
a string running through it
with the sound of a breath

lights are still there from
long ago when
they were not seen

in the morning
it was explained
to me that the one

we call the morning star
and the evening
star are the same